# 12 Progressive Solos for Snare Drum

## by MORRIS GOLDENBERG

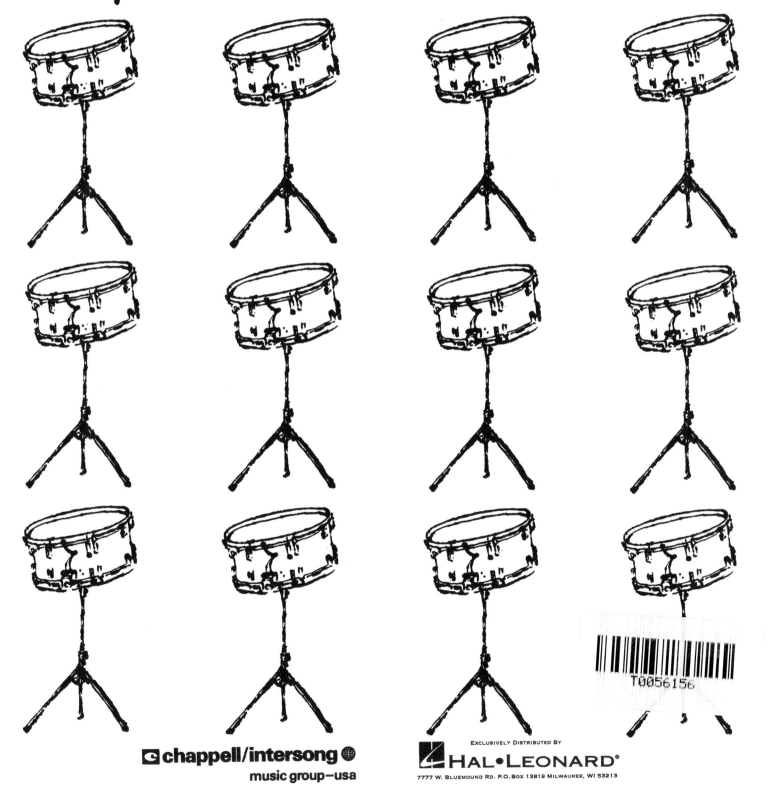

chappell/intersong ◉
music group—usa

EXCLUSIVELY DISTRIBUTED BY
HAL•LEONARD®
7777 W. BLUEMOUND RD. P.O. BOX 13819 MILWAUKEE, WI 53213

T0056156

# CONTENTS

# Easy

# Left Light March

MORRIS GOLDENBERG

# March For Two Drums

MORRIS GOLDENBERG

← with snares
← without snares

Moderato ♩=122

# Simple Minuet

MORRIS GOLDENBERG

# Intermediate

# Farfel's Gavotte

MORRIS GOLDENBERG

# No Roll Etude

MORRIS GOLDENBERG

# Simple Simon March

MORRIS GOLDENBERG

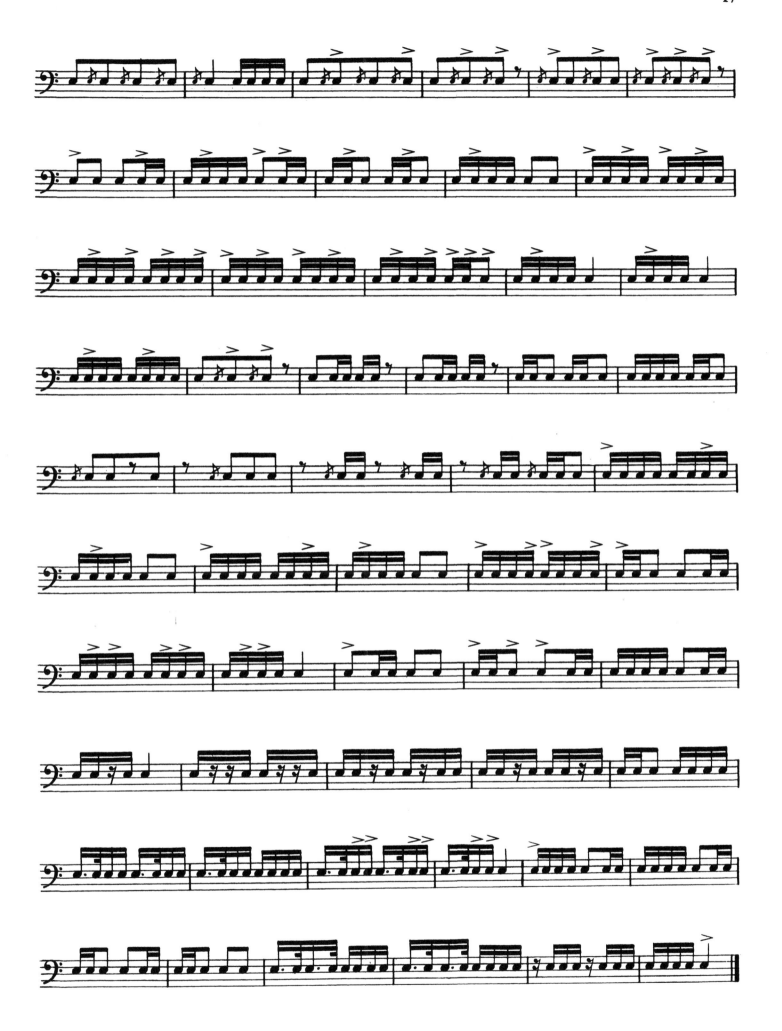

# Soldier's March

MORRIS GOLDENBERG

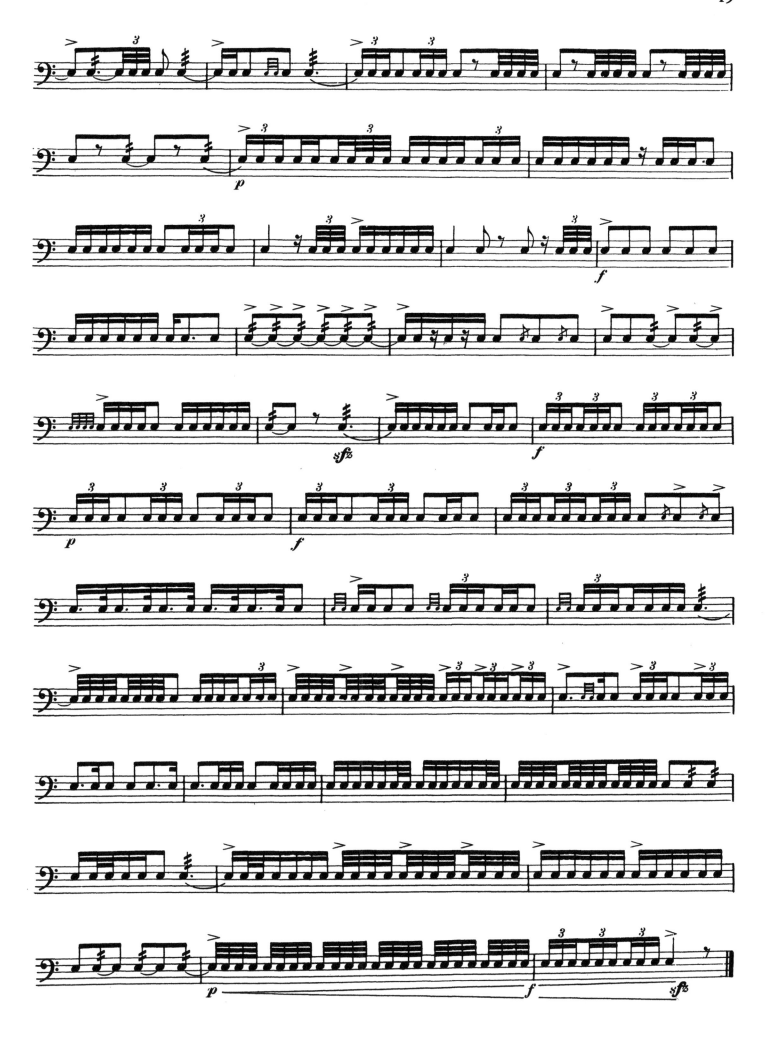

# Difficult

# 5/8 Etude 7/8

MORRIS GOLDENBERG

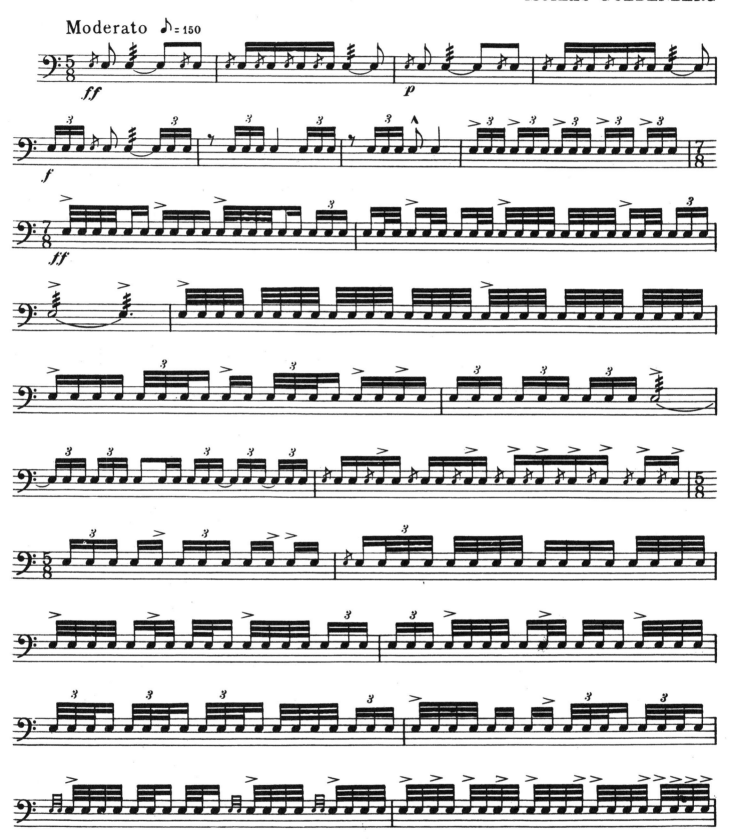

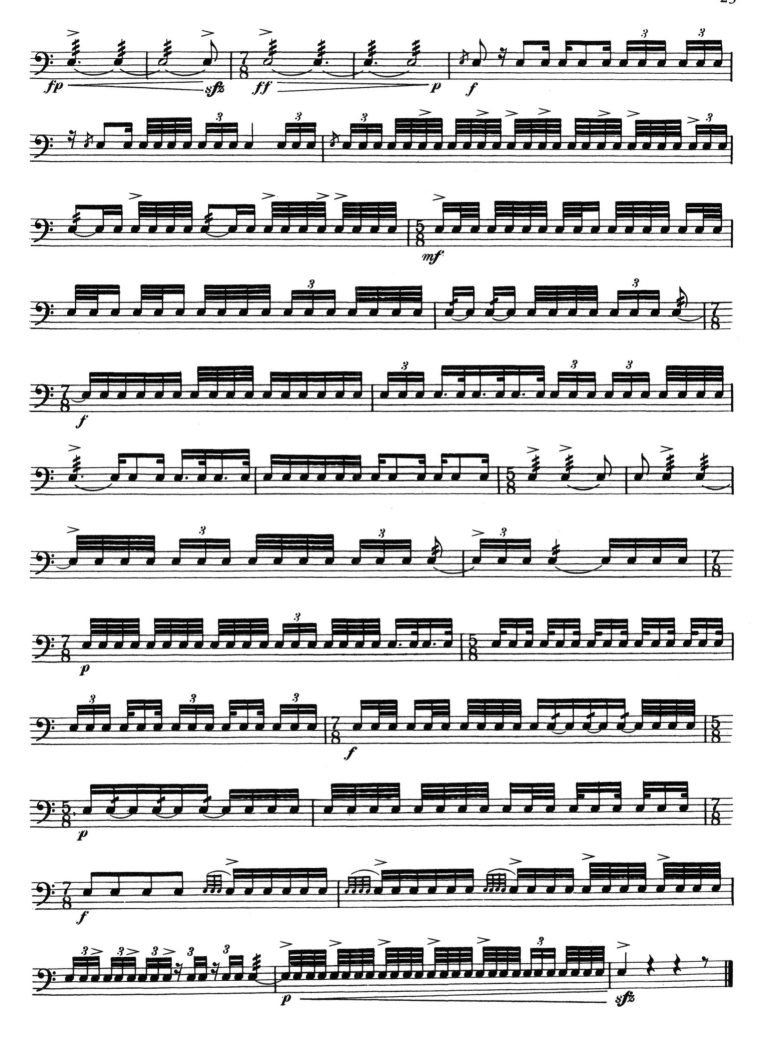

# 5/8 Romp

MORRIS GOLDENBERG

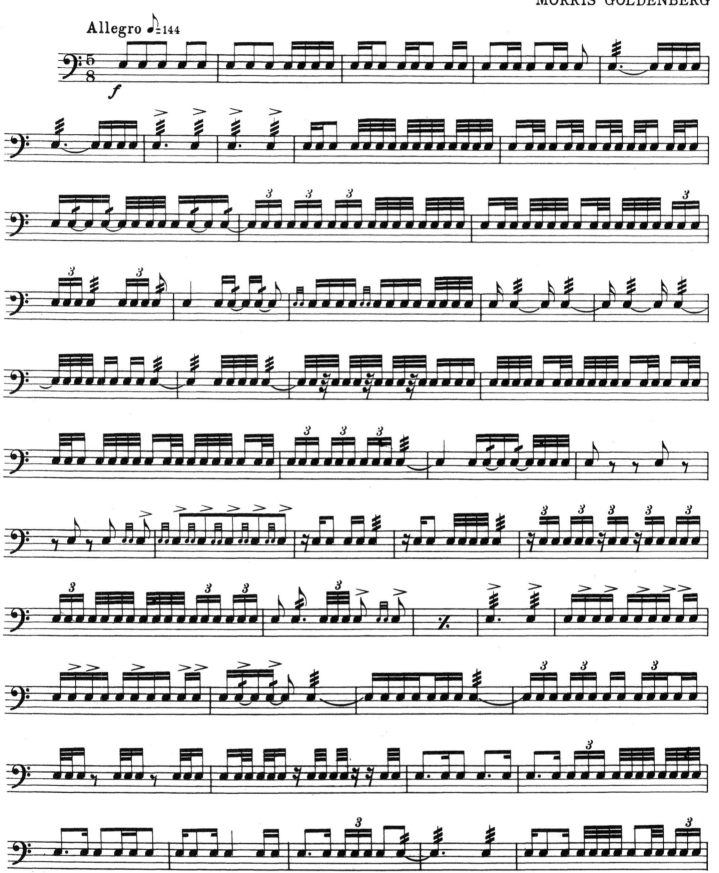

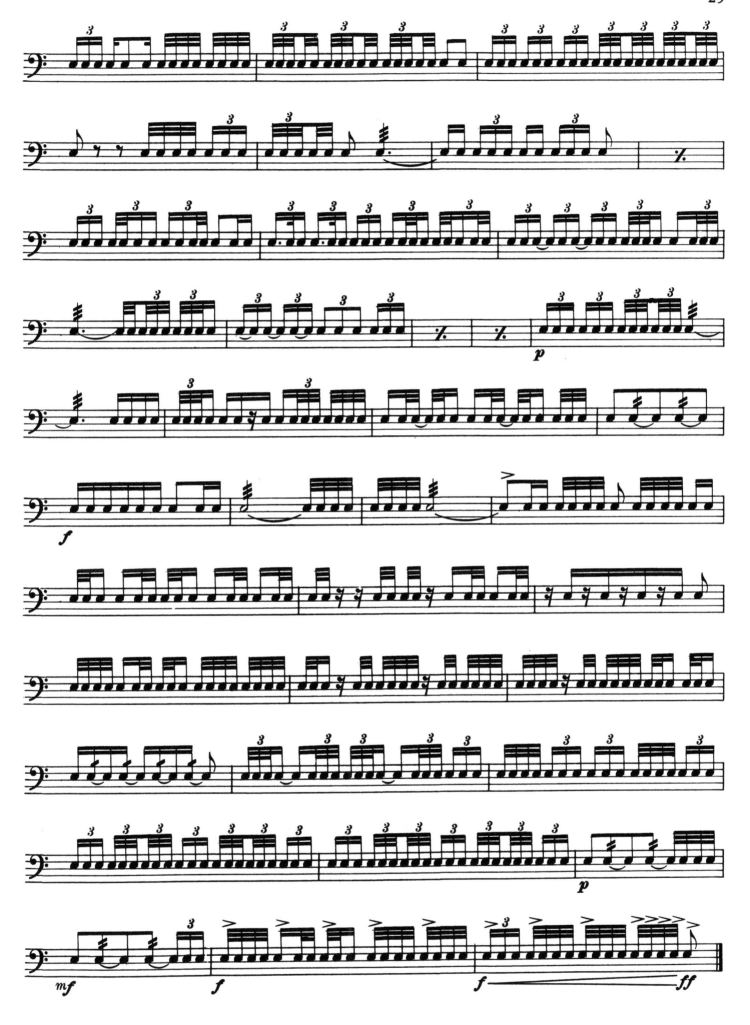

# 7/8 Romp

MORRIS GOLDENBERG

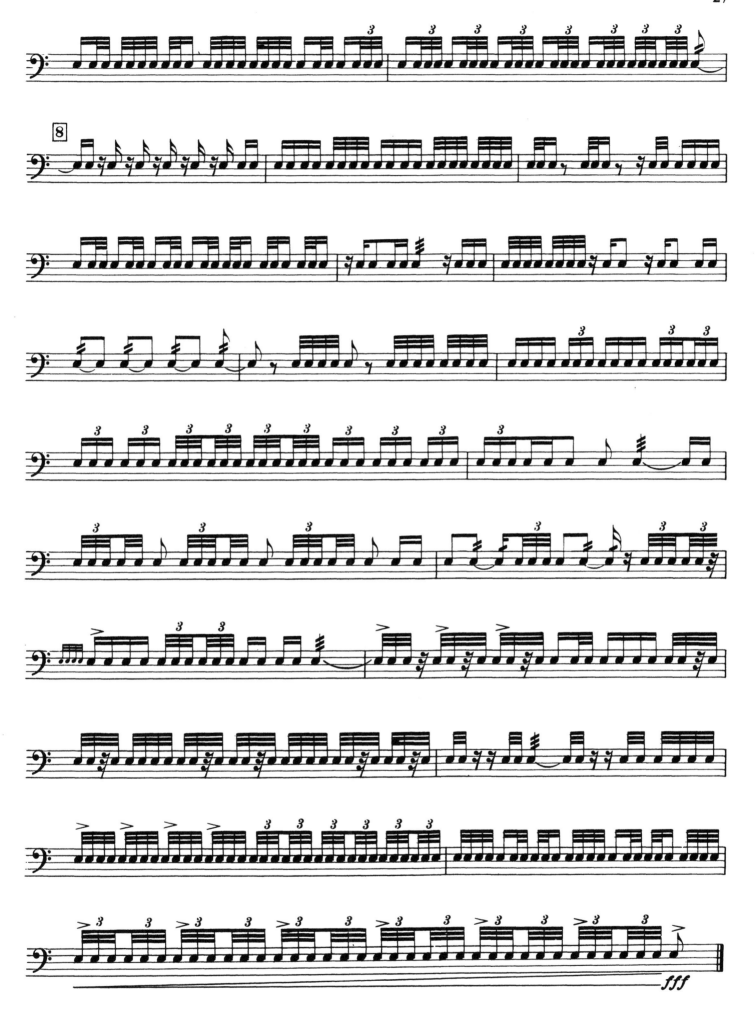

# Ramble Rumble

MORRIS GOLDENBERG

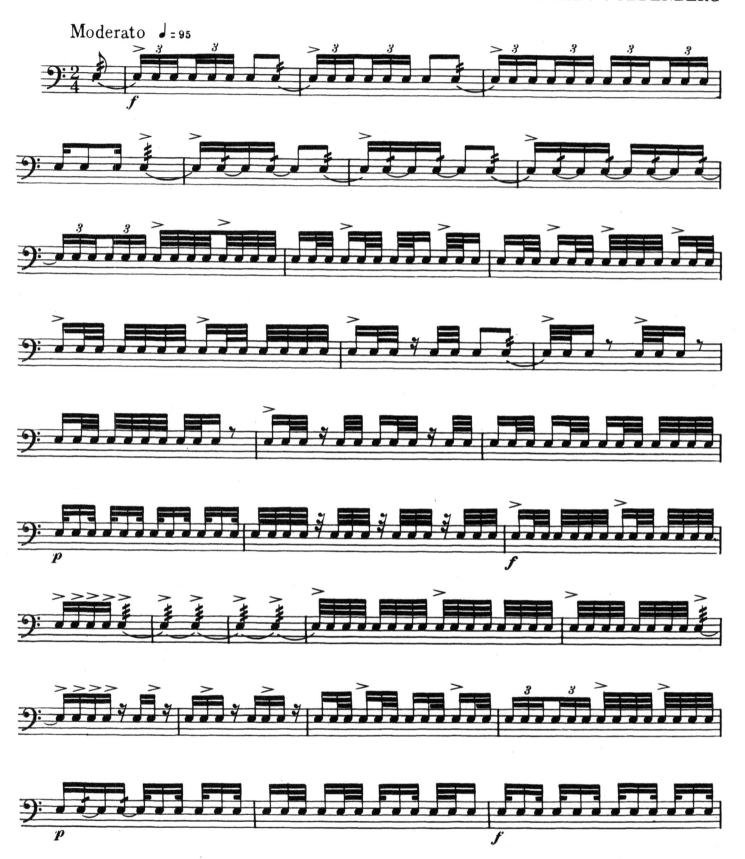

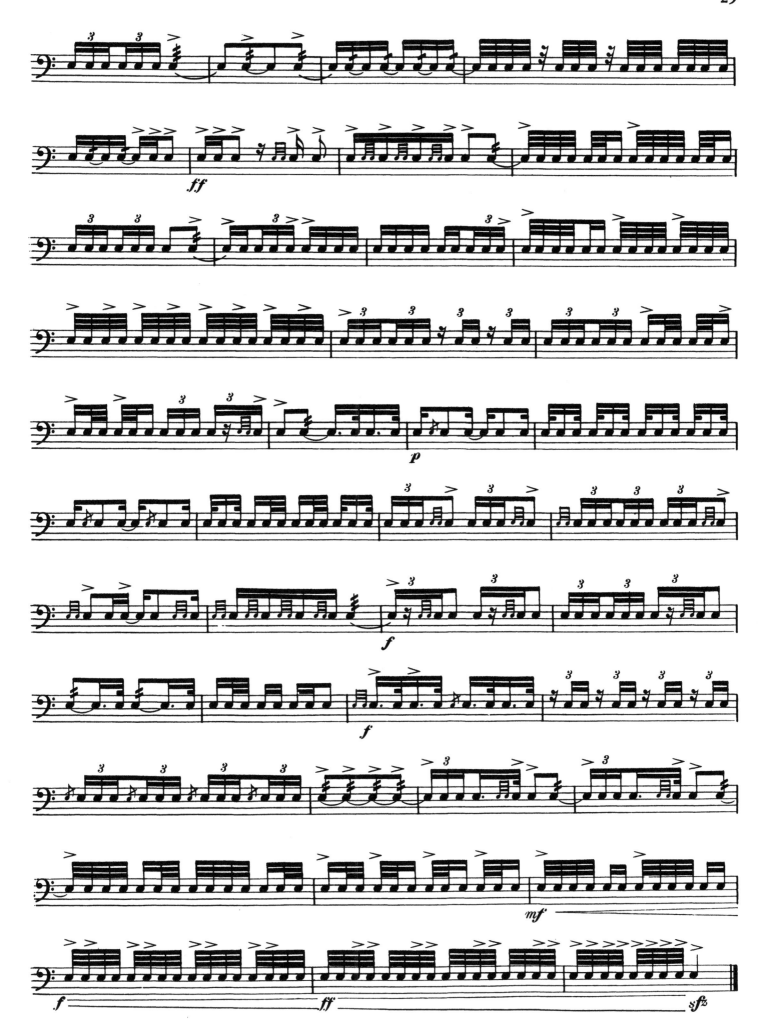

# Graduation Etude

MORRIS GOLDENBERG